921
B
C/

MONTGOMERY

ALEXANDER GRAHAM
BELL: MAN OF SOUND

DATE DUE		
Sept 2	Anna	Tutsol 3AB 214
9-29	Nadine	Kujawa 201
6-5-8	Katie	millen 203

The Discovery Books are prepared

under the educational supervision of

Mary C. Austin, Ed.D.

Reading Specialist and

Lecturer on Education

Harvard University

A DISCOVERY BOOK

GARRARD PUBLISHING COMPANY
CHAMPAIGN, ILLINOIS

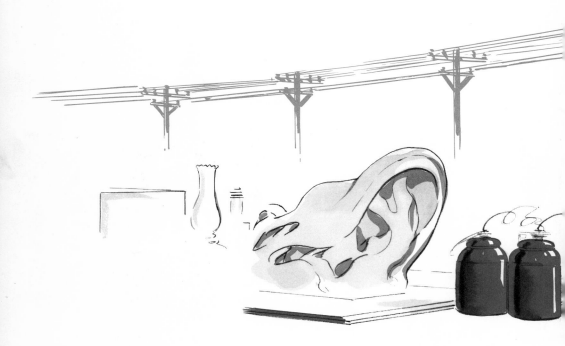

Alexander Graham Bell

Man of Sound

by Elizabeth Rider Montgomery
illustrated by Gray Morrow

921
B

Contents

Alexander Graham Bell: Man of Sound

Chapter *1*

A Name of His Own

"Mother, I want a name of my own," said Aleck.

It was 1857, in Edinburgh, Scotland.

Mrs. Bell did not look up from the picture she was painting.

Again Aleck said, "I want a name of my own. I want to be somebody myself."

The ten-year-old boy spoke clearly. Yet his mother did not hear him. Mrs. Bell was growing deaf.

Aleck's dark eyes clouded. He ran his fingers through his thick black hair. He went close to his mother and put his hand on her shoulder. Mrs. Bell looked up at her second son and smiled lovingly.

For the third time Aleck said, "I want a name of my own, Mother."

This time Mrs. Bell answered. "But, dear, you have a fine name. You were named for your grandfather. Alexander Bell is a famous teacher of speech in London, you know."

"That's just it, Mother," Aleck replied. "Grandfather and I have the same name and the same birthday, March 3. When anybody says 'Alexander Bell' they mean Grandfather and not me. I want a name that will mean only *me*."

Again Mrs. Bell smiled. She began to put away her paints. "You may choose a middle name for yourself if you wish. Your father was named for your grandfather, but he has a middle name."

Aleck nodded. Father was Alexander *Melville* Bell. He, too, was a teacher of speech.

"I shall be different," Aleck said to himself. "I shall be a musician, not a teacher."

"Whatever you call yourself, you will always be my dear Aleck to me," said his mother. "I couldn't ask for better sons than my three boys."

Aleck kissed her. He thought once again what a pity it was she was losing her hearing!

"Now go and practice your piano lesson," his mother said. "An old friend of your father's is coming to dinner, Mr. Alexander Graham. I want you to play for him."

Aleck repeated the name to himself. "Alexander Graham." Then aloud, "Alexander Graham *Bell*." It had a fine sound.

"That's it!" cried Aleck. "That's what I'll call myself. I will be Alexander Graham Bell. Then when I'm a famous musician people will know it is me and not my grandfather or father."

As far back as he could remember, Aleck had been interested in sounds. The apartment on Charlotte Street in Edinburgh often rang with happy sounds.

There was music and laughter. And there were fine voices reading aloud.

His mother loved to play the piano, and all of the Bells liked to sing. Nearly every evening they sang together. Mrs. Bell's mother often came down from her rooms upstairs to hear the fun.

But sound wasn't everything in Aleck's life. He and his brothers had a museum. They collected wild flowers, beetles and bones of small animals. Aleck wanted to know about everything. He didn't want to be *told*. He wanted to find out things for himself.

As Aleck got ready to meet Mr. Alexander Graham, he repeated his new name to himself. "Alexander Graham Bell." That was a good name. It would be his very own.

Chapter 2

The Talking Machine

"Father is home!" shouted Edward.

Aleck jumped up from the piano. Melville closed his book. All three boys ran to the door. Aleck stopped on the way to touch his mother's shoulder.

"Father is home," he said. He held his lips against her forehead as he spoke. She could hear better when he did that.

Mr. Bell greeted his family lovingly. "It is good to be home," he said.

"London is a fine city, but it is such a big place. I like Edinburgh better."

"Tell us about your trip," cried the boys. "What did you do? What did you see?"

Mr. Bell laughed. "There is too much to tell all at once. But I will tell you about the most interesting thing I saw. It was a talking machine."

"A talking machine!" cried Melville.

"Did it really talk?" asked Edward.

"How did it work?" asked Aleck.

"I don't think I will tell you how it worked," their father answered. "It wasn't a very good talking machine, anyway. I think you boys could make a better one."

Aleck and Melville looked at each other. Make a real talking machine?

How could it be done? They did not look at Edward. He was too little to have any ideas.

Mr. Bell went on talking. "I'll bet you can make a machine that talks. After all, you know more than most boys do about speech and how it is made."

Aleck and Melville nodded. They knew all about their father's work on speech. He had worked out a way of teaching people to make sounds and words. They did not have to understand the words to speak them. Mr. Bell called his plan "Visible Speech." It had ten signs. Each sign meant a certain way of placing the lips or tongue. A person could make the right sounds by following the written signs.

"You know the parts of the body that are used in speaking," Mr. Bell went on.

Again the boys nodded. The lips, the tongue, the lungs, the vocal cords or voice-box—yes, they knew all that. It would be fun to try to make a talking machine.

So the two older Bell boys set to work. They decided to make their talking machine like a real person.

"I'll make the head," said Aleck to his brother. "And you can make the throat and the lungs."

The boys became very interested in their work. Mrs. Bell had trouble getting them to stop for lessons. But they were always ready to stop for meals.

Aleck shaped a head out of wax. Inside it he put a tongue made of rubber stuffed with cotton. He made teeth and a nose too. He made lips of wire, covered with rubber.

Melville made a windpipe out of a tin tube. He made vocal cords with sheets of tin. For the lungs he made bellows, like fireplace bellows.

At last the talking machine was finished. The family gathered to see it. Melville worked the handles of the bellows hard and fast. This sent air into the tin vocal cords and made them move. Aleck opened and shut the lips of the machine with his hands.

"Ma-ma!" said the machine. "Ma-ma!"

"It talks!" cried Edward. "It is a good talking machine."

18

"It is, indeed," agreed Mr. Bell. "It's a much better talking machine than the one I saw in London. I'm proud of my boys."

"Let's put it in the hall," Aleck said to Melville. "Let's fool Grandmother."

The boys moved their talking machine out of the room. Again they worked the bellows and the lips. Again the machine said, "Ma-ma!"

Grandmother's door opened. "I hear a baby crying," she called. "What is wrong with it?"

Aleck and his brother laughed and laughed. What a good joke that was on Grandmother!

Chapter **3**

When I Grow Up

Old Alexander Bell looked at his namesake. Aleck was fourteen now, and tall and thin. He was handsome, with dark eyes, black hair and pale skin.

But the old man did not like what he saw. "You must have some new clothes," he said. "You can't spend a year with me looking like that."

Aleck looked down at his heavy clothes and thick shoes. What was wrong with them? Boys always wore clothes like these in Edinburgh.

"In London boys wear fine suits and carry canes," Grandfather told him. "My tailor is coming today. We will order some proper clothes for you."

Aleck did not like his new clothes. But he wore them to please his grandfather. He had to! Grandfather Bell gave away Aleck's old clothes. But Aleck never liked the tight-fitting pants. And he hated the top hat and the cane.

Aleck soon learned there was something else about him that his grandfather did not like.

"You have not had proper schooling, my boy," the old man said. "You do not know Latin or Greek."

"But, Grandfather!" cried Aleck. "I'm going to be a musician. I don't need to know those things."

Grandfather Bell shook his head. "Music is all right for fun. But you will be a teacher of speech when you grow up."

Aleck did not say anything. But he was sure his grandfather was wrong. He planned to be a famous piano player, not a speech teacher.

However, he soon changed his mind about what he wanted to be. It was not the lessons in Latin and Greek which made him change. It was his grandfather's library.

Alexander Bell had a fine library. There were many books on speech and on Shakespeare's plays. There were also books about sound. Aleck became very interested in these books. He read all he could find about sound and speech.

By the time the year in London was over he knew that he did not want to be a musician, after all. He wanted to teach speech. Especially he wanted to teach deaf people to speak. He wanted them to enjoy the wonderful world of sound.

However, Aleck did not tell old Mr. Bell that he had changed his mind.

Back in Edinburgh, Aleck took his place in the family again almost as if he had never been away. He played the piano for his mother every evening. She could scarcely hear anything now. She liked to watch Aleck play, and she could feel the vibrations of the music.

Aleck joined in the family singing and reading. And he helped his father with his work on "Visible Speech."

One night Mr. Bell invited some people to see how "Visible Speech" worked. These people did not believe written signs could tell a person how to speak. So Mr. Bell planned to show them.

Everyone gathered in the living room. Then Aleck and his brothers were sent into the hall. The door was closed.

"We are ready," said Mr. Bell to his guests. "Tell me words you want my sons to say. I will prove that they can read my signs."

One of the guests suggested a Chinese word. Mr. Bell had never heard it before. But he took up his pencil. He drew some signs on a sheet of paper. He showed the paper to his guests. Then he called Melville.

The boy came into the room. His father handed him the paper. Melville looked at the signs. Then he spoke the Chinese word correctly. Everybody was amazed.

Another guest said a French word. Again Mr. Bell wrote some signs. This time Aleck was called. He looked at the signs and repeated the word correctly.

All evening the guests took turns suggesting words. Not once did any of the boys make a mistake.

Finally one of the men asked, "Does it have to be a real word? Can it be an animal cry?"

"Certainly," answered Mr. Bell. "Any sound you wish."

So the man roared like a lion. Mr. Bell wrote down some signs.

This time it was Aleck's turn. At first he was puzzled. He frowned. Then he opened his mouth wide. He roared like a lion.

How the guests laughed!

"I believe you now, Professor Bell," said one of the guests. "Your 'Visible Speech' is a wonderful plan. People of any country can talk to people of any other country."

Aleck looked at his silent mother. "Even if they cannot hear the words," he thought, "people can still talk if they know 'Visible Speech.'"

Chapter *4*

Tuning Forks
and Teaching

Aleck looked around to be sure nobody could see or hear. Then he showed Melville the ad in *The Scotsman*.

"This is what we've been looking for," he exclaimed excitedly. "This Mr. Skinner wants two pupil teachers for his boys' school in Elgin."

Melville read the ad. "Do you think he would take us? You aren't even sixteen yet, and I'm only eighteen."

"I'm old enough to teach," Aleck said. "I will be a good teacher. Let's write to the man."

"He would want to know of someone who knows us," said Melville.

"We'll give him Father's name," said Aleck. "Professor Alexander Melville Bell of Edinburgh sounds important. The man will think we are all right if Professor Bell knows us."

So the boys wrote to Mr. Skinner. They asked for jobs as pupil teachers in his school in northern Scotland. They gave Mr. Skinner their father's name and address.

A few weeks later Mr. Bell came into the house with a letter.

"I don't understand this," he said. "I have a letter from a Mr. Skinner.

He asks me if I know of two teachers, Alexander Graham Bell and Melville Bell. What made that man think that my sons are teachers?"

Aleck and Melville looked at each other. Their faces grew red. They told their father what they had done. "We want to be teachers," Aleck said. "This seemed the best way to begin."

Mr. Bell laughed. "What do you think you could teach?" he asked.

"We know we could teach speech," said Melville.

"And I can teach music," Aleck said quickly.

Mr. Bell laughed again. But he talked to his wife, and they decided to let the boys teach for a while. Mr. Bell wrote Mr. Skinner a long letter.

A few months later Aleck went to Elgin alone as a pupil teacher. Melville stayed in Edinburgh to help his father.

Aleck felt grown-up now. He was over 100 miles from home. He was only sixteen, but he was earning his own money. And he liked teaching.

"Teaching is my life work," he thought. "I will always be a teacher. Soon I will begin to teach the deaf."

But Aleck was not satisfied with just teaching. He wanted to learn too. Soon after he went to Elgin he began to experiment with sound.

He used a tuning fork. This little steel fork moved back and forth when it was struck. The movement, or vibrations, made a certain tone. Aleck studied the sound it made.

Then he bought other tuning forks. Each one gave a different tone. He wanted to make them all vibrate together. He fastened a battery and magnets to the tuning forks to keep them vibrating.

Aleck wrote letters home about his experiments. "When three tuning forks vibrate at once," he wrote, "it sounds almost like a human voice!"

For five years Aleck went on teaching and studying in Scotland and England. Then three dreadful things happened.

His younger brother, Edward, died of tuberculosis. Soon afterwards Melville died of tuberculosis too. And then the doctors found that Aleck was suffering from the same lung sickness. They said he did not have long to live.

Doctors did not yet know the cause of tuberculosis or how to treat it. Mr. and Mrs. Bell believed that the cold winters were to blame. They decided to move to a milder climate.

Aleck was 23 when they moved across the ocean to the town of Brantford, Ontario, in southern Canada. For a year he did no teaching. He did little but sleep and rest and eat, and experiment with tuning forks. He made friends with the Mohawk Indians who lived nearby. They taught him their language and their war dance. Later they took him into their tribe, and even made him an honorary chief.

By the end of a year Aleck was well. His parents were very thankful that they had moved to Canada.

Chapter 5

Aleck Turns Inventor

Mr. Bell had just returned from Boston. He had been giving talks on the use of "Visible Speech."

"Do you feel well enough to teach, Aleck?" he asked.

"I feel fine now," Aleck answered. "I would love to teach again."

"Then I have an idea," Mr. Bell said.

Mr. Bell had talked at the new Boston School for the Deaf. Miss Sarah Fuller, head of the school, wanted him to come back and teach there. But he had already promised to teach in Canada. Would Aleck like to go in his place?

Aleck would! "When do I start?" he asked eagerly.

Schools for the deaf were a very new thing. Only a few years before, deaf children were put in special "homes." In these "homes" they learned to "talk" only with their hands. They saw only other deaf children. They lived in a silent world.

But a few people like Miss Fuller believed that deaf children could be taught to make sounds and to speak.

They could live with their families. So the Boston School for the Deaf was started.

Aleck was 24 when he went to Boston to teach in the School for the Deaf. He was a good teacher.

Soon other teachers wanted to learn "Visible Speech." Aleck opened a school for teachers. Now he was very busy, teaching both children and teachers. He spent summers and holidays with his parents in Canada. But he did not rest much. He was always experimenting with sound.

The Bells had many parties. Professor Bell would often give readings from Shakespeare's plays. He did magic tricks. Aleck played the piano. Sometimes he sang.

Often Aleck started strange games. He would hand a friend a toy balloon. "Speech is just a motion of the air," he said. "Hold this balloon tightly against your chest. See if you can feel the vibrations of the music through it." Then he played the piano.

Or he might ask guests to put water in their ears and listen as he sang. "Sound is different when the waves go through water," he told them. "Can you hear the difference?"

Guests always did what Aleck asked. But they began to think he was a little odd.

While he was teaching in Boston, Aleck met two deaf children who were to be important in his life.

George Sanders was five years old.

He had been born deaf. His father asked Aleck to teach him to talk. The little boy went to live with Aleck. In a few weeks he could make sounds. Then he began to say words. Mr. Sanders was very grateful to Aleck.

Aleck was 26 when he met Mabel Hubbard, a lovely sixteen-year-old girl. She had lost her hearing when she was four, but she had learned to read lips. For a while Aleck taught her "Visible Speech." Then he turned her over to another teacher in his school. Mabel's parents were grateful to Aleck. They often invited him to their home.

Aleck was very busy teaching, but he was never too busy for experimenting with sound. Often he worked late into the night.

When he made a new discovery, he got very excited. He would leap around the room in the war dance his Mohawk friends had taught him.

Soon Aleck's experiments led him to a great idea. He explained it to Mr. Sanders, George's father.

"I think I can make a multiple telegraph," said Aleck. "It will send several messages at once."

"That's a wonderful idea," said Mr. Sanders.

The telegraph had come into use about 30 years before. But only one message could be sent at a time.

"If you can invent a multiple telegraph, it would make a lot of money," Mr. Sanders said. "But how can you do it?"

Aleck explained his idea. Mr. Sanders did not understand all of it. But he believed in Aleck.

"I will help you," he said. "I will pay your expenses while you work on this invention."

A few weeks later Aleck was visiting in the Hubbard home. After dinner he sat at the piano playing for the family.

"Do you know that I can make the piano sing by itself?" he asked.

The others looked surprised.

"Listen," said Aleck.

Aleck pressed the pedal down. Then he sang, "Do!" Softly the piano made the same tone. Then he sang, "Re!" And the piano sang it too.

"What makes the piano answer you?" asked Mrs. Hubbard.

"My voice makes the air move back and forth, or vibrate," Aleck explained. "Each tone makes it vibrate at a certain speed. Fast vibrations make a high tone, and slow vibrations make a low tone."

Mrs. Hubbard nodded. She understood that.

Aleck went on. "The vibrations made by my voice move through the air to the piano string. Then the string vibrates in tune with them."

Mabel could not hear the sounds Aleck was talking about, but she could read his lips. She smiled at him.

"That is very interesting," said Mr. Hubbard. "But what good is it?"

Aleck's dark eyes began to shine. "It means I can make a multiple telegraph.

It will send several messages at once. Each message will be tuned to a different tone."

Aleck talked on and on about the multiple telegraph.

"I will help you," said Mr. Hubbard at last. "I will pay your expenses while you work on this invention."

Aleck shook his head. "Mr. Sanders has already offered to do that."

"I will talk to Mr. Sanders," said Mr. Hubbard. "We will share the expense."

And that was the way they worked it out. The three men signed a paper. Mr. Sanders and Mr. Hubbard agreed to pay all the expenses of Aleck's invention. In return, each would get a share of the money the invention earned.

Chapter *6*

I Can Hear You!

Now Aleck began to experiment in earnest. In the daytime he taught deaf children and teachers of the deaf. Half the night he worked on his invention. But he had a very hard time with it. He knew little about electricity. And his hands were clumsy with batteries and wires. He needed someone to help him.

Soon he found the right man. Thomas Watson, who worked in an electric shop, began to help him with his invention.

Watson's hands were quick and clever. He could make anything Aleck asked him to. The two young men worked well together. They became good friends.

One evening as they worked on the multiple telegraph, Aleck stopped to rest.

"Watson," he said, "I have another idea. I think it will surprise you."

Watson smiled. Nothing that Aleck Bell could say would surprise him! Aleck was an amazing young man.

"I think I can make a machine that will let us *talk by telegraph!*" said Aleck.

Watson's eyes opened wide. Talk by telegraph! That *was* surprising. It was an impossible idea. Yet the young inventor seemed to believe he could do it.

"The air changes when a sound goes through it," Aleck went on. "Sound waves make the air change."

Watson nodded. Aleck had often explained that to him.

"I think that sound waves can make electricity change too. If this can be done, I can telegraph any sound, even speech!"

Aleck picked up a pencil and began to draw. "I want you to make a machine like this, Watson. Then we can try out my idea. We shall see if I am right."

The idea of talking by telegraph became very interesting to the two young men. They almost forgot the multiple telegraph.

Both Mr. Sanders and Mr. Hubbard thought Aleck should try to finish that invention first. Then he could turn to the talking telegraph. So Aleck went back to work on the multiple telegraph.

But he could not give up the idea of a talking machine. He worked longer and longer hours. So did Thomas Watson. Sometimes they worked all night in their attic workroom. Aleck wrote long letters to his parents about the experiments.

On the night of March 10, 1876, they were trying out a new idea on their new machine, the talking telegraph.

Aleck sat in front of the machine. On the bench beside it were wires, tools, and acid for the batteries.

"Go into my bedroom, Watson," he told his friend. "See if any sound comes over the wire now."

Watson went into Aleck's bedroom. He stood close to the machine at the end of the wire.

Suddenly he jumped with excitement. Over the wire he heard Aleck's voice loud and clear. "Watson, come here! I want you!"

Watson dashed into the workroom.

"I heard you!" he shouted. "I could understand what you said!"

Aleck was so excited! He forgot why he had called his friend. He began his Indian war dance. Watson joined him.

The two young men leaped and stamped around the attic, yelling loudly.

At last Watson looked at the young inventor. "What happened to your clothes? What made those holes?"

Only then did Aleck remember that he had upset acid on himself. It had burned his leg and his clothes and he had called for help. But he was so happy that his talking telegraph really worked that he did not even feel the pain.

Chapter 7

It Is Called a Telephone

"Aleck, you must do it!" said Mabel Hubbard. "You must show your talking machine at the Centennial Exhibition!"

The Centennial was a huge fair, held in Philadelphia that summer of 1876. It celebrated the birthday of the United States. The nation was now 100 years old. There were many exhibits in the fair to show how the United States had grown in the past 100 years. Many new inventions were shown.

Aleck looked hard at Mabel. Nobody would have known by looking at her that she was deaf. She had learned to speak well, and she could read lips. How Aleck wished his mother would learn lip-reading! She could understand very little that was said to her now.

Aleck wanted to please Mabel. They loved each other and wanted to get married. But he would not go to the fair, even to please her.

"I haven't time to go to the fair," he answered. "A teacher cannot leave his school."

"But this is important, Aleck!" cried Mabel. "If your machine is shown at the fair, people will see it. They will want to buy it and use it. You could make money from your invention."

How Aleck wanted to make some money! He could not marry Mabel until he had money to live on. Mr. Sanders and Mr. Hubbard had paid his expenses on the multiple telegraph and the talking machine. But they could not be expected to give Aleck money to get married.

"You *must* do it!" Mabel repeated. "It is our great chance." She was a sweet, gentle girl, but she could be very firm.

At last Aleck gave in. He agreed to take his talking machine to the fair. But he would come back to Boston in time for his Monday morning classes.

Aleck's talking machine was put in a corner of the exhibit hall. Few saw it.

Few people were interested. Saturday was a very hot day. People wanted a cool place to sit down. They did not want to look at crazy new inventions.

The judging took place on Sunday. The fair was closed while the judges looked at the exhibits. Aleck waited for the judges to come. He hated to sit and do nothing. He was hot and tired, and he had a headache.

Then he saw the judges coming toward him. His face brightened.

But they stopped *before* they got to his exhibit! "It is too hot to judge any more exhibits today," said one of the judges. "Let's go home. We'll judge the others tomorrow."

Aleck's heart sank. By tomorrow he would be back in Boston!

Then a man in the group of judges saw Aleck. It was Dom Pedro, Emperor of Brazil. He had met Aleck in Boston. He had visited his school for the deaf.

"Why, it's Professor Bell!" exclaimed Dom Pedro. "How are the deaf children getting along without you?"

"I must go back to Boston tonight," Aleck answered. "I do wish the judges would look at my invention before I go."

"Of course they will look at it!" cried Dom Pedro. And the judges came to Aleck's table.

"What do you call your invention?" one of them asked.

"I call it a telephone," Aleck answered. "It is a talking machine. I will show you how it works."

"Hold this thing to your ear and listen," he told Dom Pedro. Then Aleck ran across the exhibit hall to the other end of the wire.

Dom Pedro held the thing to his ear as Aleck had told him. He listened. Suddenly he heard words coming over the wire.

"*'To be or not to be. That is the question.'*"

Dom Pedro looked up at the judges. "It talks!" he cried. "I can hear words!"

The judges took turns listening. They were amazed. They went to the other end of the wire and talked into the telephone. It *was* a talking machine! They gave Aleck's invention the prize.

Aleck was very happy. Now maybe he could get married.

Chapter *8*

A Useless Toy

Nobody seemed to want to buy Aleck's telephone after all. Nobody wanted to use it. Everybody said it was a useless toy.

Aleck tried to explain how useful it would be. It would send messages across town, without paying a messenger to take them. It would call a doctor when someone was sick. It would invite guests to parties.

Nobody would listen. Aleck could not find a way to make money out of his invention.

Then Aleck took Watson to visit his parents in Canada. They strung wires from Brantford to another town eight miles away. They talked over the telephone to each other. They let people listen, and they let people talk to each other over it.

Aleck gave shows with his telephone, both in Canada and in Boston. He would hire a hall. When people were seated, he talked about his telephone. He talked through it to Watson and Watson talked to him. People listened and watched. They clapped and smiled. But most of them still thought the telephone was a useless toy.

By the next year, however, a few people saw that the telephone could be useful. They began to believe it was an important invention. Mr. Sanders and Mr. Hubbard formed the Bell Telephone Company with Aleck. They started to make telephones and put them into use.

Mr. Sanders and Mr. Hubbard thought that all the money the telephone earned should go to Aleck. But the young inventor did not agree.

"Without your help I could not have made the telephone," Aleck told them. "I got the idea for it while I was working on the multiple telegraph."

Finally Mr. Sanders and Mr. Hubbard agreed to take a share of the money.

Now that Aleck was making money, he and Mabel could get married.

They were married in 1877, when Aleck was 30 and Mabel was 20. They went to Brantford to see Aleck's parents. Mrs. Bell met them at the door. She had an oatcake in her hand. She broke it over Mabel's head. How surprised Mabel was at this queer greeting!

"This is the way we do in Scotland," Aleck's mother explained. "Now you will never go hungry in your husband's house, my dear."

Mabel smiled happily. She would not mind going hungry as long as she was with Aleck.

Soon after they were married, Aleck and Mabel went to England. Aleck wanted to interest the English people in his invention.

Queen Victoria asked to see the talking machine. So Aleck went to her palace. He set up a telephone from one room to another.

Queen Victoria listened while Aleck explained how it worked. She wanted to try it herself. But she did not understand that she must hold it close to her ear.

Aleck forgot it was not good manners to touch the Queen. He put his hand on her arm. "Your Majesty, you must hold it close to your ear. You will not be able to hear unless you do."

Queen Victoria turned and looked at the bold young man. But she did not scold him. Instead she did as he said. And how surprised she was to hear the voices coming over the telephone!

She asked to keep the telephones which had been set up in the palace.

Aleck and Mabel were very happy. Their first daughter had just been born. And now that the Queen had shown some interest in the telephone, it would soon be a great success.

Chapter *9*

The Great Mr. Bell

Aleck and Mabel returned to Boston in November, 1878. They learned that the telephone was making money at last. Mr. Sanders and Mr. Hubbard were very happy. Mr. and Mrs. Bell were very, very proud of their son.

However, the Bell Telephone Company soon began to have trouble. Many men began to copy Aleck's invention. They said they had invented the telephone.

More than six hundred lawsuits were brought against Aleck. But each time Aleck was able to prove that he had invented the telephone first. The letters he had written to his parents and Mr. Hubbard about his experiments helped him to prove it.

Aleck was very happy. His invention was a success. He had two little daughters now. There was no danger that Mabel or the children would ever go hungry.

The Bells had moved to Washington, D.C., but they spent their summers in Canada, at Brantford or Cape Breton. They all enjoyed swimming, boating, and hiking. No matter where he was, Aleck kept on experimenting and working on new inventions.

As the years passed the Bell Telephone Company grew and grew. People who had said Aleck's invention was a useless toy changed their minds. They began to use the telephone every day. Soon they could not see how they ever got along without it. Telephone lines were strung from city to city.

In 1915 a line was put all the way across the United States. Aleck was asked to be the first to talk on it.

Aleck sat in an office in New York City. And across the country in San Francisco, Watson sat in another office.

Aleck looked at the black telephone in front of him. How different this telephone was from the first one on which he had talked! He thought of all that had happened since that night.

What a long way he had come! Then
he was very poor. Now he was rich.
Then he wanted to get married. Now
he had a lovely wife, a fine home, two
grown-up daughters and several grand-
children. Then he was interested in
helping deaf children. Now he was still
interested in work with the deaf. Then
he had worked day and night. Now he
still worked day and night. Mabel had
a hard time getting him to go to bed.
He always had so many ideas he wanted
to work out.

"Ready, Mr. Bell," said a telephone
man. "Ready to talk to San Francisco."

Aleck thought for a moment. What
should he say to Watson? Then he
knew. He lifted the receiver.

"Are you there, Watson?" he shouted.

"Yes, Mr. Bell, I'm here," Watson's voice came over the long, long wire.

"Watson, come here," said Aleck. "I want you."

Over the telephone Aleck could hear Watson laugh. "I'd be glad to come, Mr. Bell," he said. "But it would take a week to come to New York from here!"

Many honors came to Aleck in later years. People all over the world honored him for his invention of the telephone.

Aleck never stopped working and experimenting. As long as he lived he kept on inventing. He invented things to help make airplanes successful. He invented a kind of air conditioning. He invented a tool which helped doctors.

He invented a way to change sea water into drinking water. He invented the comic strip. These and many other inventions were made by Aleck Bell during his long and active life.

In 1922 Alexander Graham Bell died at the age of 75. But his name lives on. He will never be forgotten as long as people use his invention, the telephone.

And he will never be forgotten by people who cannot hear a sound over the telephone. Deaf people will always be grateful to him for the work he did for them throughout his life.